I0541687

TEN POINT PROGRAM FOR ORTHODOX LIFE

Translating Orthodox Christian Ideals Into Daily Life

by Deacon Charles Joiner, PhD

2025

Copyright © 2025 by Deacon Charles Joiner, PhD
ISBN: 979-8-9987486-1-5

All rights reserved. No part of this book may be reproduced in any form or by any electronic or mechanical means including information storage and retrieval systems without permission in writing from the publisher, except by a reviewer, who may quote brief passages in a review.

For permissions contact Fr, Deacon Charles Joiner at cjoiner@mac.com.

For more information about how to live the Orthodox way of life, visit our website www.OrthodoxWayofLife.org or contact Fr. Deacon Charles Joiner at cjoiner@mac.com or write to Saint George Greek Orthodox Cathedral
406 N Academy St
Greenville, SC, 29601
864-233-8531

Index

By living the Orthodox Life you put Christ's commandments and way of life deep into your consciousness. You learn to deal more effectively with stress. You release reserves of untapped energies. You transform anger. You heal relationships. You leave behind painful memories and live a life fully in the present. You develop unsuspected capacities for insight and understanding. You learn to love more fully than you thought possible. You discover your unique contribution to life. You walk a path towards eternal life in Paradise.

Introduction

The final goal of man is communion with God. The path to this communion has been precisely defined: faith, and walking in the Commandments with the help of God's grace.

Saint Theophan the Recluse

While it is true that the Orthodox way of life is not the normal way of life for most people in our society, it is a most practical life for married people with families faced with the challenges of careers. In fact, it is the way of living that will make your life less stressful and more meaningful.

The Orthodox Way of Life is NOT a monastic way of life. Even though monasticism was part of the early church, we are not required to live this most honored lifestyle. Only a few are called to this style of life. We do, however, have the same goals. Like the monks we seek holiness and union with God, but we are called to live in the world with our families. The principles of our spiritual growth are the same no matter which path we chose.

Most of us never take the time to reflect on the purpose of our lives. Often we don't do this until someone we love departs from this life unexpectedly. During this moment of grief, our soul has our attention and we begin to think about what life is all about. In one way, life is about death. We all know this is where we are headed, but we too often refuse to think about this seriously because of the unknown and the fear it presents.

The purpose of life taught by the Apostles and the Church Fathers is one of finding union with God. Jesus came to save us and to open the gates of heaven for us. He showed us how to live through His teaching and example. He showed us that we have nothing to fear in death.

To begin, you must have faith in God and accept His love for you. With a little faith, you can begin to live the Orthodox way of life outlined in this booklet. This way of life is given to us by Christ Himself through His

Church. It is a proven way of life that WILL bring you closer to God. As you come closer to God, you increase your capability to deal with any difficulty you may face. You increase your ability to live according to the virtues.

These ten points presented here are only an outline on how to find union with God.

However, if you follow them you will be led to everything you need to know.

Study each one of them and examine your current life. Then seek ways to make the necessary changes in your life to incorporate them. Always pray for God's help in this.

1. Praying Daily

Prayer is the foundation of the Orthodox way of life. It is a dialogue between you and God. It unites your soul with God. It is through prayer that you unite with God and receive the gift of His grace to aid you in overcoming your passions and living life based on love. Through prayer you also learn to control the distractions of your mind, allowing you to become more watchful and focused in your daily activities. Prayer is the key to entering a life based on the virtues.

How do you pray? First, establish a regular time and a private place. You should have a specific rule for both morning and evening. Don't try to "wing it." This is not a relaxation exercise, but a path of communion with your God. You will benefit from having a specific set of guidelines that you follow each time with no excuses for shortcutting them. In your rule, incorporate standing, prostrations, kneeling, making the sign of the cross, reading, and at times singing. Use prayer books and written prayers. The Orthodox prayer books are filled with prayers that have been well-tested and used for hundreds of years. Prayer does not need to be a creative activity. Above all, you need to be sincere. Keep your awareness in your heart and concentrate on the words of the prayer. Once you establish a rule, always keep it. Work with your spiritual Father on this.

You begin praying by focusing your consciousness in your heart and forcibly gathering there all the powers of your soul and body. Before you start your prayers, take time to quiet yourself and to concentrate your energies in your heart. Christ says, "Enter into thy closet and ... shut thy door" (Mt 6:6). Remove all activities that could disrupt your inner descent. Set aside, to the best of your ability, all of your problems of the day and your worries for tomorrow. This is not a time for thinking or worrying. When you are preparing to pray, stand, sit or walk a few minutes and steady your mind to concentrate on God. Reflect on who it is that you will be addressing. Remember, it is God Himself, the Creator of All, with whom you are about to talk. Try to hold in your heart a feeling of humility and reverent awe. If you are able, make some prostrations before you begin.

As you begin to pray, enter into every word of the prayer. Bring the meaning of the words down into your heart. Do not rush through the prayers like you are in a hurry to finish them. Let the words of the prayer slowly drop into the depths of your heart with humility and awe of God. You need to slow your mind down so you can concentrate solely on your prayer. It's somewhat like driving a car. When you are going 90 miles per hour down the highway, you may feel exhila- rated, powerful and in control. But, at high speeds things can go wrong quickly.

But, when you slow down and drive at a speed of twenty-five miles per hour, the car handles easily and if someone makes a dangerous maneuver you can easily avoid it. The mind works the same way. You want to train it to slow down so it will not cause you an unneeded accident and you can open your heart to God's presence. So, in prayer say the words slowly so you can gain the full meaning of them and allow them to penetrate your consciousness and to bring to your heart feelings of love and reverence for God. Beware of the tendency to rush to com- plete them hurriedly. When this happens you have turned your prayer into an obligation, another task to complete, and it is no longer true prayer. Don't worry if you catch yourself doing this. It is normal at first. Just stop, slow down, and then continue after asking God's forgiveness and help. You will eventually find the right pace for yourself. Also, study the prayers before you use them so you know the meaning of each word. Eventually you will want to memorize them.

After you begin to recite your prayers, you will find that your mind will want to wander. This means you are still driving at a high speed. Don't be concerned about this; it is natural due to our overactive minds. Work constantly to improve your ability to concentrate your attention on God and your prayer. When your mind does wander, be gentle with yourself. Think of God and how He loves you and go back to recite again what you said while your mind was elsewhere. Bring yourself back to concentrate on God and the words of the prayer. Sometimes it helps to say your prayers out loud for a while to help you concentrate. The mind is quite skilled at trying to do more than one thing at a time. But in reality, you only concentrate on one thing at a time. You can easily be deceived by the mind as it leaves prayer to focus on other matters. These wanderings of the mind show you the dimensions of your busy life and where you need to find ways to make it quieter so you can be always mindful of God. Prayer is NOT the time to focus on these worldly activities, because this will only further distract you from prayer. Work to concentrate your attention more and more each time you pray.

Each day you will gain in your attentiveness during prayer.

When you finish your prayers, stand for a few moments. Consider to what your prayer life commits you. Try to hold in your heart what has been given to you. Treasure it for a few moments.

It is important to make your prayer life one that is a firm rule, a desired habit, and not something that is done occasionally, sporadically or casually. Pray each and every morning and evening for fifteen minutes at a minimum. Your prayer rule should include specific prayers (See the back of this booklet for an example of a beginning prayer rule). Commit to doing your rule each and every day, just like you are committed to daily personal hygiene tasks such as brushing your teeth. You don't forget to do them each day. You need to make prayer a similar habit, one that you never forget. Just like brushing our teeth is essential for the health of our gums and teeth, prayer is essential for the health of our soul. Persistence and patience in prayer will prepare you for God's grace to work within you.

2. Worshiping and Participating in the Sacraments

Those who are well have no need of a physician, but those who are sick. But go and learn what this means: I desire mercy and not sacrifice. For I did not come to call the righteous, but sinners, to repentance.

Jesus Christ (Matt 9:12-13)

Along with our personal prayer we need to participate in corporate prayer, or prayer that is offered during a worship service. Worship in the Church is an essential part of a life in Christ. The Church is the body of Christ on earth. When we all gather together for worship, we are united with the angels and saints in our prayer to worship and glorify God.

We enter the place of worship humbly, knowing that we are not worthy to be in union with God, but, we enter with a strong yearning, with zeal, to come closer to Him. We enter with the understanding that through the sacraments, teachings, and practices of the Church we will grow spiritually. While we may find social benefits of joining the Church, this social activity is not the purpose of the Church. It is better described as a spiritual hospital where we come as individuals in need of spiritual healing. By joining the assembly of believers in Jesus Christ, we find this healing and are shown a step-by-step process whereby we can receive God's helps to come closer in union with Him.

The Holy Spirit works in the Church and provides spiritual nourishment through the sacraments of the Church. It is important to participate in them because they have been given to us by Jesus Christ Himself for our spiritual health.

Major Sacraments of the Church Holy Communion

The Divine Liturgy is the most important service and it provides us with a kind of spiritual medicine: Holy Communion. This is why you should come to church each Sunday to be renewed and strengthened through participation in Holy Communion. Here the Body and Blood of Christ are offered to the members for the forgiveness of their sins and eternal life. You need to regularly partake of this gift that God offers to us all for our spiritual benefit. This is why one of God's commandments is to participate in worship each Sunday. As you develop your personal prayer life you will no longer see this as an obligation, but as something you want and need to do for your spiritual benefit. Make regular attedance at the Divine Liturgy a part of your prayer rule and learn how to properly prepare and participate regularly in the sacrament of Holy Communion.

Most assuredly, I say to you, unless you eat the flesh of the Son of Man and drink His blood, you have no life in you. Whoever eats My flesh and drinks My blood has eternal life, and I will raise him up at the last day. For My flesh is food in- deed, and My blood is drink indeed. He who eats My flesh and drinks My blood abides in Me, and I in him.

Jesus Christ (John 6:53-56)

Holy Confession

Confession is also an important sacrament for your spiritual growth. By your participation in this sacrament you renew your Baptism and are freed from all your sinfulness in the eyes of God. Don't fall into the trap of thinking you do not sin. None of us lives without sinning. This sacrament involves standing before the icon of Christ with a contrite heart, asking God for forgiveness for all the times you have not lived up to what He has made you capable, with the priest by your side as your witness. You should do this at least two times a year.

Holy Unction

In this sacrament, you are anointed with oil that has been blessed to give you strength in healing physical and spiritual sickness. It is offered to all during Holy Week and on request at other times.

Marriage

In the sacrament of marriage, a couple stands in front of God, commits themselves to a union and are united as one in the eyes of God. This is a path set forth for the benefit of their spiritual growth and union with God.

Ordination

In this sacrament, the priesthood is given to an individual, and he is endowed with the spiritual powers to carry out his work.

Baptism and Chrismation

He who believes and is baptized will be saved (Mark 16:16).

Baptism is the beginning of the Orthodox Christian life, where one is cleansed from all past sins and sealed with the Holy Spirit. It is how one joins the Church and becomes part of the body of Christ and becomes able to participate in all the Sacraments for spiritual benefit. Chrismation is the anointing of the Holy Chrism, which is the seal of the Holy Spirit. It is a sacrament normally done right after Baptism.

Holy Communion, Confession and Holy Unction are interrelated because they serve for the healing of the body and soul. Make participation in worship and the sacraments of the Church a regular and integral part of your life.

2. HONORING THE LITURGICAL CYCLE

The Church in Her Holy wisdom offers us a cycle of fasting and feasting. This cycle is based on the life of Christ. The key is to learn to follow it, to participate in it, and not to allow other activities in life to be viewed as more important. Follow the prescribed fast times. Participate in the major feast days of the Church. Plan your schedule to make this a reality.

The Church year begins in September. This initiates a period of preparation for the celebration of the Nativity and Baptism of Christ. As we approach Christmas there is a 40-day Nativity Fast. Participate in it and consciously prepare for this important spiritual event. This will counteract the commercial madness we normally experience at this time of year. Following the Nativity, there is a feasting period (the twelve days of Christmas) capped by the celebration of Theophany or the Baptism of Jesus on January 6th. Celebrate with others during this period. Make an effort to turn your life into this cycle of fasting and feasting.

Shortly after the Theophany, there begins the period to prepare us for the most important event, Pascha or Easter. It begins with a preparatory three week period prior to the Great Fast of Pascha, called the Triodion. Use this period and the teachings designated for the four Sundays during this period to help you get into the right attitude for the Great Fast of Lent. When Lent begins, fast to the best of your ability, keeping in mind the fasting guidelines of the Church for this period. The fast leads up to Holy Week, which is the most intense period in the Church Liturgical cycle. Holy Week takes us through the Passion of Christ and His Crucifixion and leads us to His glorious Resurrection and victory over death. Take time off from normal activities this week to participate in these beautiful services. You will find new meaning in the Resurrection as you break the fast with the joyous announcement of the Resurrection at midnight on the first dawning of the feast day of Pascha. Following

Pascha, plan for another period of feasting and celebration with family and friends. Next we await the Ascension of Jesus, which comes 40 days after Pascha. Ten days later, this is followed by the coming of the Holy Spirit at Pentecost, celebrating the time when the apostles were empowered to carry forward the teachings of Jesus to all parts of the world. We can think of this as the birth of the Church here on earth.

In addition to these large cycles, there is a weekly cycle and even a daily cycle. During the week we should fast on Wednesdays and Fridays. Make a commitment to remember to control your eating habits by restraining them on these two days in remembrance of our God.

In addition to the normal morning and the evening daily prayers, the Church prays additionally on what are called the Hours: midmorning, noon, mid-afternoon, and at the setting of the sun. As you mature in your prayer life you can make time for such prayers throughout the day.

The liturgical cycle provides for periods where you can more intensely focus on your spiritual needs. The time of Great Lent is most important for this. It provides a time to withdraw from your busy life, to limit your normal activities, to increase your time in prayer and reading of Scriptures, and to concentrate on your inner self, seeking what is most important for your soul to become united with God.

Here are the 12 major Feasts of the Church:

September 8	Nativity of the Theotokos
September 14	Elevation of the Holy Cross
November 21	Presentation of the Theotokos
December 25	Nativity of Jesus
January 6	Epiphany (The Baptism of Christ)
February 2	Presentation of the Lord
March 25	Annunciation
Sunday before Easter	Palm Sunday

Easter — Pascha

Forty Days after Easter   Ascension of the Lord

Fifty Days after Easter   Pentecost

August 6 Transfiguration of our Lord

August 15   Dormition of the Theotokos

Arrange your schedule so you can participate in the Divine Liturgies held on these days. Of course, don't forget to make every Sunday a time for participating in the Liturgy as well.

It will provide a challenge for you to give priority to the schedule of the Church and not to allow it to become secondary to all other activities. Always keep in mind that union with God is your aim in life and that through your full participation in the Liturgical cycle of the Church you will be helped to continually grow closer to Him. This commitment is difficult in a society which does not pay any attention to the liturgical cycle of the Church. But if you plan ahead, even if you have a very busy schedule, just like you can fit in your physical fitness activities, time with your children and other non-work related activities, you can find ways to build your schedule around the key events in the Church's liturgical cycle.

Think about how you plan to fit other activities into your schedule, like a vacation, school, or sports, and make the same effort for these spiritual events.

4. Using The Jesus Prayer

Lord Jesus Christ, Son of God, have mercy on me a sinner.

This prayer has the potential to transform your consciousness and bring you closer to God. It is a prayer rooted deeply in the tradition of the Church. It is a prayer to be repeated over and over, many times. You can begin to develop the use of this prayer by incorporating a number of repetitions in your daily prayer rule. A simple prayer, you can learn to say it everywhere and at any time. In fact, your aim should be to make it an unending prayer. In this way your whole life becomes a life of prayer.

Recognize, however, that this prayer is incredibly difficult to practice even though it seems very simple. In its practice, you continually recite it so that it permeates your heart and focuses your mind, predisposing you to follow God's will instead of your own ego directed will.

Start by repeating it for ten minutes in the morning or evening. Begin by saying it out loud or at least by moving your lips. Eventually you will repeat it mentally, but start with a verbal prayer. Add more repetitions, slowly building up the time you are able to concentrate on the prayer. When your mind wanders, bring it back to the prayer. Concentrate, but do not be harsh on yourself. This is not something you will master with your self-will. Ask God to help you conquer the restlessness of your mind. With persistence, humility and patience, the practice of this prayer will prepare you for God's grace to work actively within you.

Along with saying this prayer as part of your prayer rule, try to say it whenever you can. You can do this while walking, while waiting in the doctor's office, in line at the post office, or while waiting to board a plane. You can say it when doing dishes or yard work. You can say it when you are stressed, afraid, or nervous. When you become angry, repeat this prayer over and over until your anger subsides. Do this whenever your mind is agitated, and you will find that it will calm your mind. When you do say it, be sure to think of God and His endless love and seek His mercy.

The practice of the Jesus Prayer is different than Buddhist, Hindu or Sufi practice. In Buddhism, a common practice is to constantly repeat a mantra such as "Om mani padme hum." The aim of Buddhism is to free oneself from all suffering and attain what the Buddha called "Nirvana" or the perfect peace of mind. This peace of mind is achieved through various meditation techniques. The Buddha never taught about any form of God. Many practice this form of meditation to gain calmness in their lives. Sufism is a branch of Islam that also employs forms of meditation. Sufi scholars define Sufism as "a science whose objective is the reparation of the heart and turning it away from all else but God." In meditation they aim to reach an awareness of their oneness with the universe, believing that in doing so they can attain fundamental truths that are within us, but often remain hidden. They do not believe that Jesus is God, but view Him as only a prophet. In Hinduism the chief aim is to gain release from the cycle of reincarnation caused by karma—the consequences of past actions, in this or in previous lives! This is achieved though meditation techniques. This release leads to some kind of absolute Truth. Many of these approaches have been adapted by our modern culture to serve as means of relaxation or ways to lessen the stress of our over-active lives. They form the basis of the "New Age" spiritual movement. They are taught without any specific aim of repentance, nor the purpose of doing the will of God, nor of seeking union with Christ.

The use of the Jesus Prayer is done with an attitude of repentance and humility seeking an encounter with the living Christian God, Jesus Christ. We may gain benefits of relaxation or reduced stress, but this is not the aim of our effort. Union with God is. It is NOT a mantra to simply quiet the mind. You will also gain this benefit if you learn to repeat it hundreds of times, but it is important that you truly feel contrition for your sinfulness and seek God's mercy as you repeat it. All prayer is about a personal relationship with God.

Many Orthodox Christians use a prayer rope to aid in concentration as they repeat the Jesus Prayer. Prayer Ropes come in a great variety of forms and sizes. Most prayer ropes have a cross woven into them or attached to mark the "end," and also have some kind of marker after each 10, 25, or 50 knots or beads. There are many forms of prayer ropes, some knotted of wool or silk, or other more elegant or simpler materials. At the time of your regular prayer, when you pray following your rule of prayer, hold the prayer rope with your hand between the thumb and the index finger and move from knot to knot each time you say the prayer. Do this until the number of repetitions in your rule have been completed.

Just as it is impossible to fight battles without weapons, or to swim a great sea with clothes on, or to live without breathing, so without humility and the constant prayer to Christ it is impossible to master the art of inward spiritual warfare or to set about it and pursue it skillfully.

Saint Hesychios

For more on the Jesus Prayer go to our website on prayer:
www.OrthodoxPrayer.org.

5. Slowing Down and Ordering Your Life

Modern life is a too-busy life. We are all driven to work faster and faster and more and more efficiently. Our kids are involved in multiple activities with demanding schedules. With all the demands of work and family, there is little time left for reflection and prayer. As a result we can become insensitive to the needs of others and feel the burden of stress. Such a fast-paced life makes us feel tense, inefficient, insecure and even superficial.

There are many ways you can slow down and simplify your life. To start the process, you can begin by getting up earlier. (Which means you also need to go to bed earlier.) When you get up in the morning, your first activity should be prayer. At least thirty minutes is desirable (start with 15 minutes and work up to 30 minutes). This includes prayers of thanksgiving, repentance and intercession. You also should include the practice of the Jesus Prayer at this time. After you have prayed and you have taken care of all your personal hygiene needs, you should plan time for your other responsibilities such as getting the kids ready for school. You should allow time for a leisurely breakfast. Help others in your household get off to a peaceful start of the day. You do not want to start the day being pressured by time. Remember, harried people create harried people and calm people create calm people. If you don't start the day with calmness there is not much chance that the rest of the day will be calm.

The easiest way to find this time is to examine the way you spend time with the different forms of media such as the television, the Internet or the cell phone. Most likely, television is the biggest culprit. Give up just one of your programs and you will automatically have an extra hour to start the day off on the right foot. Media usage places a huge burden on all our lives. A recent survey by Nielsen Media Research shows that the average person spends more time than ever in front of the TV, over 133 hours a month. In addition, we spend on average another 26 hours using the Internet. Both of these have shown significant increases over the prior year. Now the phone is connected to the Internet and we can even spend another 3 hours watching video and TV on the phone. The mo- bile phone is becoming a significant use of our time as well as being an instru- ment that diverts and scatters our attention. So, this is the prime area to look to reallocate your use of time so you can make time to be with family and friends, to help others in need, or to make time for your daily prayer, attend worship services and most importantly to get a calm start each day. If you watch TV or surf the Internet to get relief from the tensions of the day or because of boredom, prayer will bring you even greater benefits.

To change the pace of your life, eliminate some activities from your "To Do" list. Identify those things that do not promote your spiritual growth and conflict with the Orthodox way of life. At work you carefully set priorities and make sure you are doing those things that are the most important. Do the same for your personal life. At the end of the work day you need to separate yourself from the work activities. If you leave work at work, then you can better enjoy your friends and family when you are off work. You will be able to take time to listen to your children and your spouse. The end of the day should be one of slowing down until it is time for your regular period for prayer, to read some Scripture, or to read from the works of the Church Fathers. Have your conversation with God, and then go to bed focused on His love and great mercy. Organize your life so this period after work is a leisure time detached from all work activities.

Do not confuse slowing down with being lazy or slothful. These are quite different things. Laziness leads to procrastination and inefficiency. A lazy person will not make the effort to organize time for prayer. As you slow down you will find you pay more attention to the details. Concentrate on even the smallest things you are doing. The quality of your actions will improve in everything you do.

Jesus constantly warns against having anxiety about material things, even food and clothing. God knows and provides everything you need, but most likely you have taken your needs and exaggerated them beyond what are your basic necessities. To follow Jesus, He asks you to abandon your attachment to possessions and the priority you are placing on things of this created world, and to take on a simpler lifestyle focused on God where you are not encumbered with excessive demands to accumulate material things for your happiness. The key is a balance. Plato and Aristotle taught mankind, hundreds of years before Christ, that the ideal is a golden mean, which implies a path through life that is neither burdened with excess nor with deprivation. By slowing down or simplifying our lives we are not talking about being less productive or rejecting the whole of this material world. We are simply being more effective, balanced, and doing what we do with much greater care, which includes the exercise of the moral imperatives that God has laid down for us.

There is no magic formula to slowing down and simplifying your life. The possibilities are endless. Start by clarifying your priority values. Then make a list of all your activities. Record them over a week's time. Take time to reflect on what you have recorded and determine which ones fit with your priorities. Think about what you can eliminate to put a different priority in place in your life. Begin to consciously reengineer your pattern of life. Experiment with ways to slow down and simplify and you will find yourself coming closer to God in your daily activities. Through your prayers, seek God's help in this task.

6. Being Watchful

Watchfulness is the action to guard us from our automatic reactions to thoughts stimulated by our senses. It is being attentive to your inner self. The Greek word that is translated as watchfulness is "Nepsis". It comes from "nepho," which means to guard, inspect, examine, watch over and keep under surveillance. Watchfulness has been described by Elder Ephriam of Philotheou as "the axe which shatters the large trees, hitting their roots. When the root is struck, it doesn't spring up again."

Saint Hesychios sees watchfulness as follows:

Watchfulness is a continual fixing and halting of thought at the entrance to the heart... If we are conscientious in this, we can gain much experience and knowledge of spiritual warfare.

He shows us that this involves an effort to intercede on our thoughts, forcing them to be examined, to shine the commandments of our Lord on them. He emphasizes the importance of this by calling it warfare. We know in warfare we need to have effective weapons that are stronger than those of the enemy.

Another church elder from modern times, Paisios, tells us about some of the consequences of not being watchful.

When our soul lives carelessly without watching over its thoughts, it will consequently fill up with dirty and sly thoughts.

As a result, people start developing psychological problems which gradually pile up. Some people, while they are found in this situation and come face to face with the problem itself, they do not realize it, and thus are unable to humbly confess to their spiritual father their fall. Instead, they look for a "secular" solution and consult a psychiatrist, who will inevitably prescribe medication. The only solution is to become aware of the problem and confess it to a spiritual father and then humbly follow his advice.

In our days, people have lost control over their lives, and they do not know what they are doing. The reason being, that they do not wish to be guided; they want to live undisturbed, following their own free will, which will eventually bring their total destruction. When man uses his freedom and independence without taking into consideration his human weakness, he becomes deceived; he experiences and interprets everything by using his own logic. Instead of God's grace, human logic rules his life, and his mind is in confusion. This is terrible.

Elder Paisios

It is essential to develop self-control over the inner workings of our mind. Most importantly, you can learn to harness the actions of your mind which tends to run wild and unchecked. This unbridled condition leads you to rely on mental programming that needs to be changed if you are going to live the Orthodox life.

Being watchful means you have the necessary self-discipline to guard your inner sanctuary from being invaded by thoughts stimulated by your senses that lead you to sinful actions such as anger. It is an ability to intervene in the process of choosing how to act based on any kind of stimulus that leads to a thought. It is a capacity to intervene in real time in your thought process.

How do you experience the distractions in your mind? Reflect on the times you notice that you were distracted in your daily activities. Was it due to an argument? Was it due to having too many commitments and you could not live up to all of them? Was it a recurring worry? Did it come from a feeling of guilt? Was it sadness that distracted you? Maybe you felt lonely and began to feel sorry for yourself. Was it a fear of something? Maybe you wanted something you don't have? Each of us will have our own set of issues that are distracting us and keeping us separated from God.

A mind that is left to its own devices will remain untrained. An untrained mind is impossible to control. It will remain jumping from one thought to another just like a butterfly in a field of flowers. It will quickly jump from one flower to the another in what seems like a random pattern. To develop mindfulness or watchfulness requires ascetic disciplines, such as prayer and fasting, as well as help from the Holy Spirit.

Doing one thing at a time is a good way to become more watchful. Focus totally on each activity. Don't let your mind wander. Make this a discipline until you feel you have this capacity of watchfulness. Of course the regular reciting of Jesus prayer will help develop this ability. Ordering your life will also help you create a less distracted life situation. Participating in worship and the liturgical cycle of the church will help to keep your mind focused on God. As long as you insist on living life as if you can do many things at the same time without any regard for God, you will remain scattered in your mind and you will not remember Him when you need God the most. Slow down, order your life, and focus on one thing at a time. Turn your whole life into a prayer.

With God's help, in the context of the Church, you can train your mind to become focused and pointed so it acts more like the laser beam, with the power of the Holy Spirit.

7. Taming the Passions

Passions are initiated by our senses. If you are to become truly free and learn to live by God's will, you need to learn to control the passions that result from the way you react to your senses. For example, you may crave certain foods. When you are deprived of them you become disturbed and possibly even angry. Gaining freedom from these likes and dislikes is what we mean by taming the passions. When you are able to do this, you gain the freedom to do God's will and to love others by being less focused on your own desires. This does not mean you need to deprive yourself of good food or entertainment. Everything God created is good. It means you should enjoy what is necessary for your welfare but also forego all the indulgences based on your desires for sensual pleasure. You cannot simply ignore the passions. You need to recognize them and then train them to come under the control of your soul and mind. This is how you can live in ways that do not undermine your health, security, or freedom from sinful tendencies such as anger. With untrained passions it is like having a team of wild horses pulling your wagon. You think you are the driver, but the horses decide to go where they want. These wild horses are the untamed passions. The challenge is to harness and train your passions so they will follow your commands, just like a trained team of horses is obedient to the commands of the driver.

This task begins with acknowledging that you ARE often controlled by your likes and dislikes. Begin by learning to say no when you are being led to indulge in something you know is not good for you. Gaining discipline in what you eat is a first place to start. This is one of the benefits of the fasting we are advised to do. By choosing not to eat certain foods, you are, in effect, training your mind to be more obedient. When it becomes obedient, then it will be more capable of doing God's will. You will gain greater freedom. In the tradition of the Church, fasting was always one of the first disciplines taught after prayer. This was taught to us by Christ Himself. The first thing He did after His Baptism was to go into the desert to fast and pray for forty days. Since He was both fully human and fully divine, He had to tame His human passions.

As was discussed earlier, the Orthodox way of life involves many fasting periods and days. There is the Great Fast before Pascha; we are to fast each Wednesday and Friday; and we fast before receiving Holy Communion. You can follow the church calendar for fasting guidelines that have been established by the Church to help you in your efforts to tame your passions. Always seek the advice of your spiritual father on what is appropriate for your personal situation.

Often you find that you are stuck in a rut and so conditioned to a particular like or dislike that you cannot bear even the thought of tearing yourself free from it. It is like there is a deep groove engraved in your mind, like a rut, that you cannot get out of. You do the same thing over and over without even thinking. These ruts need to be identified and eliminated so you are free to choose. When you are stuck with following your own desires that are automatically stimulated by your senses, and your ear takes in something another person says that triggers anger in you, you are headed for conflict. At the moment when you react with anger, you are unable to love as God commands. In fact you are immediately separated from God.

Try to become observant of all your likes and dislikes and recognize the passions they trigger. This means being able to appropriately say yes and to say no as a rational choice, not based on an automatic response. The answer is not necessarily abstinence. We want to go beyond relying on abstinence, but abstinence may be necessary as a start to break a pattern that controls us. Avoidance of situations that trigger your passions is one approach, but as you develop some of the other points presented here you will be able to intervene in the moment they are aroused and choose more appropriate courses of action. You want to be able to intervene in your thought process when desires arise. This is where watchfulness and the practice of the Jesus prayer are most important. Instead of reacting like a robot, you can condition your mind to call upon the prayer to interrupt and lift you out of the rut. As you identify your main ruts, you can pray for God's help. If you maintain a regular prayer life, participate regularly in worship services and the sacraments, God will help you.

Our passions are like a pet. If you have ever had a puppy you will remember how they take a shoe or other item and chew on it and tear it apart. They growl when you try to take it from them. This is normal behavior for a young pup, but not one we want to have continue. If we do not train the puppy in the beginning, it will stay wild and even turn against us later on. Our passions are like puppies. Unfortunately many of us have grown up without properly training our passions. When we try to confront them they are not eager to cooperate. They rebel like angry pups. Controlling them becomes a difficult task but one that is essential to a virtuous life.

When you first begin to tame your passions, you may experience inner irritation. As you wrestle with them, you will find that the block is in the mind. Also, as you mature in your prayer life, you will find that you have increasing means to overcome the ruts conditioned into your mind. As you seek God's help, you will be aided in this struggle. Through regular prayer, especially repetition of the Jesus Prayer, you will even be able to create new ruts that are beneficial to the health of your soul, new patterns that are stronger than the old ones. Eventually the soul will regain its normal position of being in control. The mind then becomes a powerful and useful tool under the enlightened direction of the soul for living the life that God desires for us.

8. PUTTING OTHERS FIRST

As you begin to slow down your life, reorder your priorities, become more watchful, and gain freedom from the chains of your likes and dislikes, you will also begin to see changes taking place in your relationships.

It is selfless relationships that lead us to happiness and a life close to God. This is what Christ meant when He asked us to love our neighbor as ourselves. You cannot act as an isolated being and be close to God. When you dwell on yourself you only build a wall between yourself, others and God. Those who insist on thinking about their own needs, their wants, plans and ideas only become lonely and feel insecure. They separate themselves from God.

A powerful approach to learning to love is to practice putting others first. You can begin with your own family and close friends and coworkers. As you try to understand the needs of your spouse or best friend, and begin to consider their needs before you insist on your own, you will find that you move closer together. This kind of action weakens the negative aspect of your ego-centeredness and opens deeper relationships with others.

There is a ripple effect that begins with your closest relationships. As your closest relationships grow, you will find that those further removed will also grow closer. Your love ripples outward. At the same time you will find yourself growing closer to God. So, begin this practice with those who are closest to you.

Most of us find that we are all puffed up by our ego. We see the world based on what we like and dislike. We think everyone has the same hopes and fears, likes and dislikes that we do. Too often we expect others to behave just like ourselves. But, when they don't and they expect us to act the way they do, we run into conflicts. This is the reality of the world.

Try to allow yourself to think in the way others think, to appreciate their likes and dislikes, to look at things from their perspective. Then you will find that your relationships blossom.

The block to knowing God is the same as the one that blocks us from loving others. It is our self-will. We grow spiritually when we learn how to eliminate our self-will. This is the aim of putting others first. This is the example that Christ has set out before us. This is the accomplishment of the Saints of the Church. This is what Jesus meant when He said, *If you want to find your life, you have to lose it.* One of the two great commandments He gave us is to love your neighbor as yourself. Why? Because he wants us to be able to love Him. God is present in all of us, and when we love each other we are loving God. It is through our love of others that we can come to know the love of God.

The ability to put others first demands patience—a calm and controlled mind. This virtue only comes with a disciplined life based on a foundation of daily prayer where you gain strength to control your passions and get beyond your own likes and dislikes. Continually ask for God's mercy and His help to overcome your self-willed nature. When you are patient and able to think of the needs of others, an unkind word will not agitate you and trigger anger. As you become more watchful and your life more ordered, then you can support others even when they are angry with you.

You can practice putting others first even at work. Learn to accept that others may have good ideas even if they are different from your own. When you no longer expect everyone to be and think like yourself, and when you recognize their likes and dislikes without judgment, you will begin to build loving relationships at work. In fact, work is a great place to get rid of the sharp edges of your personality. As you learn to love in the work environment, your example will be seen by others for the benefit of all.

Some will say that putting others first will only make you like a doormat and subject you to abuse. This is not what putting others first is about. You do not automatically say yes to everything others want. What we are saying is to put the other person's welfare before your own desires, not necessarily all their wants. There are times when it is in the best interests of the other person to say no. And there are other times when we say yes even when it goes against one of our own desires, because we know it is what is best for them. This is the essence of godly love. You are putting others first when the other person's welfare means more than your own desires. It is like the love a mother naturally has for her infant child. This is the sacrifice that Christ made on the Cross. He willingly gave His own life for our salvation. Often in a relationship it is necessary to say "no" when we know it is not in the best interests of the other person and "yes" when it does not meet our own desires.

You can also mend broken relationships with love. It is the act of forgiveness that is the most powerful healing power. Forgiveness makes both parties whole. When you forgive those who have done wrong to you, you also forgive yourself for your wrongs of the past. This brings up another benefit we have in the Church: the sacrament of Confession. In this sacrament you can ask God to cleanse you of all your past transgressions, all the cases where you were not able to control your passions and master your self-centeredness. In this sacrament not only are you cleansed by the Holy Spirit, but you also gain spiritual advice, a penance, to help you overcome the passion that you find most difficult to control. When you "clear the deck," when you humble yourself before God and admit your weaknesses, you open yourself to become more understanding of the struggles of others and become more willing to forgive them. As you forgive others you are more able to forgive yourself. As you do this you will find you are more able to put others first. The result is that we all come closer to God.

9. Spiritual Fellowship

Those you spend your time with influence your thinking and behavior. If you associate with those who share your values, then they will be reinforced. You want to develop a circle of friends that lifts you up to higher ideals and to avoid those who negatively influence you. You need to look for the goodness in others when choosing your friends and consciously choose who you spend your time with on a regular basis. When you find others who share your spiritual values then you should find ways to spend more time with them.

When you are engaged in making changes in your way of life, you need the support of friends with whom you interact regularly. Seek out those who are also trying to live an Orthodox way of life, meet with them, read the same books and discuss them. Share with them in your times of entertainment as well.

A good way to develop a strong relationship with such people of like mind and values is to work together for a selfless goal. This may be a project such as reducing hunger, or working on a Church function. When you work with others on a project that does not involve any expectations of reward or recognition, you will find that your energies are multiplied and the synergy of different people is maximized.

This is the value of the Church community. It is a place where we all share the same ideals. We come together at least once a week for common worship. We can participate in Bible study and Sunday school where we can continue to learn together. We can interact in social activities as well.

In your spiritual growth you are like a tree seedling. At first a new seedling needs to be protected in a safe environment and even fenced off to protect it from the grazing animals. When it matures, however, it can survive on its own. In the beginning you too need a safe environment; your emerging Orthodox way of life needs protection. As you mature spiritually you can then enter into any company and not fear being uprooted. As your relationship with God grows, you will have less need for this protection, as you will have the Holy Spirit supporting you. You then can become a source of protection for a new emerging seedling.

The Apostle Paul sees our spiritual path as one that involves struggle and requires endurance. He says, *Let us run with endurance the race that is set before us, fixing our eyes on Jesus, the author and perfecter of faith.* He explains that we are involved in a struggle with our desires and the Spirit, *The sinful nature desires what is contrary to the Spirit, and the Spirit what is contrary to the sinful nature. They are in conflict with each other, so that you do not do what you want.* He then shows us that we need to be involved supporting each other in this struggle. *Therefore, brethren…, by a new and living way which He consecrated for us… Let us hold fast the confession of our hope without wavering, for He who promised is faithful. And let us consider one another in order to stir up love and good works, not forsaking the assembling of ourselves together, as is the manner of some, but exhorting one another, and so much the more as you see the Day approaching.* Our spiritual companionship should be of such a nature that we can strongly encourage each other.

Whom you spend your time with makes a difference. If you choose wisely, you will get the encouragement you need. If you do not, you will find you are encouraged to give up the struggle and instead seek a life of pleasure and self-satisfaction. It is a common saying that you are known by the company you keep. If you associate with those who share your values, then those values will be reinforced. When you associate with those who are also involved in this struggle, their experiences will give you knowledge and strength. They will help you expand your vision, and you will profit from their experience. Since they are also spiritual aspirants like you, they will inspire you, strengthen your resolve, elevate your aim, and enable you to progress more surely on this difficult path.

In addition to spiritual companionship, the Orthodox tradition suggests that Christians should have a spiritual father to guide them on their spiritual journey. This goes back to the earliest days of Christianity. Saint Paul points to the relationship between a spiritual guide and his spiritual children. *For though you might have ten thousand instructors in Christ, yet you do not have many fathers; for in Christ Jesus I have begotten you through the gospel. Therefore I urge you, imitate me.* He points out that this relationship involves the imitation of life and character of the spiritual father. Later in the 4th century St. Basil the Great encourages each person to find a spiritual father *who may serve you as a sure guide in the work of leading a holy life* and warns that *to say that one does not need counsel is great pride.* To risk directing your own way is risking that you will fall prey to the most powerful of all sins: pride. We can all easily be misled by our own direction and be tempted to think that we are making great progress, when we are only building up our own ego and our pride.

Each person needs a spiritual father if he or she is sincere in seeking God's will and growing in faith. The role of the Orthodox spiritual father is leading seekers along the spiritual path, helping them conquer their passions, guiding them in ways of prayer, ascetic disciplines, and participation in the sacraments and leading them to ultimate union with God.

10. Reading Scripture and Holy Fathers

What you read has an impact on the way you think. So does what you watch on TV or at the movies. Think about what you want to let into your mind to influence your thinking. Your reading should be something that will be a positive impact on your spiritual growth, that will shape your mind and orient it towards God.

To maximize the positive conditioning of your mind, you should plan to make time to regularly read the Holy Scriptures, the writings of the Holy Fathers and the lives of the Saints. You should organize your life so that you can spend at least a half hour a day for this task, maybe instead of one of the TV programs you watch regularly. A good time for this is in the evening just before bedtime, before or after your evening prayer. When you do this, you will then fall asleep with these sweet thoughts in your mind.

The spiritual life is challenging. It is like an ascent up a steep slope or mountain side. It is a long and slow pathway with joyful moments along the way. As you move along the path, you gain strength. You can begin to look back and reflect on how far you have come while still seeing that you have much further to travel. As you gain strength, you will be able to face an ever more difficult terrain as well as the uncertainty of storms that you cannot predict. It is often a lonely path, and at times it seems like you will never reach the summit.

As you face these difficulties, the readings, especially the lives of the Saints, can inspire you with courage to continue along the path. You can see that others have traveled this path before you, and with persistence and faith, they have reached much higher heights than you can now see. As you turn to those who had an intimate relationship with God, they will give you hope and kindle a spark of warmth in your heart. They will help you keep your head high and your eyes fixed on the summit ahead. They will show you that your capacity to choose, to change, and to endure is a reality. They will show you the way to wisdom and love and the potential to be able to radiate spiritual glory as you discover the uncreated light of God and find yourself in glorious union with Him.

The Bible contains the most important books to read regularly. Here are some suggestions on how to read the Bible:

Read the Bible with obedience. Remember that it is inspired by God. It is Christ Himself speaking to you. This means you need to maintain a sense of wonder along with listening without judgment. Don't take wonder for granted. Because of your familiarity or the commonness of the Bible, you can take what is written in the Bible just like any other written material and lose your sense of awe and wonder as you read it. Reading the Bible cannot be like reading a novel or the daily newspaper. Just like prayer, you need to prepare your mind to the nature of the text you are about to read. This is the Word of God. With wonder, you can open yourself to listen to what is being said. Look for the spiritual signif-icance of what is written. Remember the Bible is not a textbook, but a spiritual document. As you listen to the words as you read them, you will realize the awesome task that God has for you and His unlimited love He has for all humankind.

When you read the Bible, don't try to make up your own interpretation. Scripture is to be interpreted through the Church. Remember the story of Philip coming in contact with the Ethiopian reading the Bible in his chariot? Philip asks him, "Do you understand what you are reading?" The Ethiopian replied, "How can I unless someone guides me". This is the same attitude you should have.

Scripture is not always self-explanatory. When you are at different stages of your spiritual growth, passages will take on different significance. As you grow spiritually, the Bible has more and more to teach you. You should take advantage of Biblical commentaries of the Church Fathers to help you. This is one of the advantages of using the Orthodox Study Bible, as it contains comments to help you understand what is written as interpreted by the Church. When you read the Bible you make full advantage of your own understanding illuminated by the Holy Spirit and also make full understanding of the commentaries of the Church

Fathers. In the end when you have questions or opinions, submit them to the Church for clarification.

Your reading of the Bible should always be Christ-centered. Your interpretation should be made in light of the harmony and completeness that Jesus brought to this world. You cannot take an analytical approach and break each book or chapter into its own part. The Bible must be understood as a whole, with Christ as the bond and union.

You should also read the Bible for a personal application. Saint Mark the monk (5th-6th century) says, *He who is humble in his thoughts and engaged in spiritual work, when he reads Holy scriptures, will apply everything to himself and not to his neighbor.* Do not ask, "What does this mean?" But, instead ask "What does this mean for me?" When reading the Bible, first reflect that Scripture is a sacred history of the world from the time of Creation through the formation of the early Church. Then observe the particularity of this history where we find God intervening at specific times and places and entering into dialogue with specific individuals. After reliving this spiritual history, apply it to yourself. You need to bring these distant places and times into your own place and time and see that these stories include you.

Conclusion

To live the Orthodox life there is obviously much more to learn. You may find that you are not currently living all the ten points outlined in this booklet. Remember, being an Orthodox Christian is to be on a path of continual growth. As we come closer to God, we learn more clearly what He expects of us. As we grow closer to Him, He provides us with greater ability to practice His teachings. We are all sinners and the Church is the place we come for spiritual direction and forgiveness. In God's eyes it is never too late to change our ways. Not only does he expect us to be perfect as He is perfect, but He is most merciful to those who are the greatest sinners.

Reflect on each of these points and seek ways to include them in your current life, no matter how busy or hectic it is, and you will find that you will grow spiritually. As you grow you will find all you need to know. One caution: This is not a list to pick and choose from. It is very important to include ALL of the points in your way of life. They are interrelated. Not one of them is sufficient on its own.

If you want to learn more, you can find all the resources you need on the website www.OrthodoxWayofLife.org. You will also want to find a spiritual Father to guide you. Any Orthodox priest or monk can help guide you safely as you walk the path to Theosis or union with God.

A final thought from our Lord and Savior Jesus Christ:

Every one who acknowledges me before men, I also will acknowledge before my Father who is in heaven; but whoever denies me before men, I also will deny him before my Father who is in heaven. He who loves father or mother more than me is not worthy of me; and he who loves son or daughter more than me is not worthy of me; and he who does not take his cross and follow me is not worthy of me.

Peter replied to Jesus, *Lo, we have left everything and followed you. What then shall we have?*

Jesus said to them, *Truly, I say to you, in the new world, when the Son of man shall sit on his glorious throne, you who have followed me will also sit on twelve thrones, judging the twelve tribes of Israel. And every one who has left houses or brothers or sisters or father or mother or children or lands, for my name's sake, will receive a hundredfold, and inherit eternal life. But many that are first will be last, and the last first.*

From Matthew 10:32-33; 37-38; 19:27-30

BEGINNING DAILY PRAYER RULE

Here is an example of a beginning prayer rule that you can use for your morning and evening prayers. It is recommended that in the beginning you use the traditional Orthodox prayers as handed down though the ages. As you repeat them and then memorize them they will take on deeper and deeper meaning to you. Be sure to consult with your spiritual father on a rule appropriate for you.

In the name of the Father, the Son and the Holy Spirit. Amen.
Glory to You our God, Glory to You.

Trisagion Prayer
Heavenly King, Comforter, the Spirit of Truth, present in all places and filling all things, Treasury of Goodness and Giver of life: come and abide in us. Cleanse us from every stain of sin and save our souls, O Gracious Lord.

Holy God. Holy Mighty. Holy Immortal Have mercy on us.(3)

Glory to the Father, and the Son and the Holy Spirit, both now and forever and to the ages of ages. Amen

All Holy Trinity, have mercy on us. Lord, forgive our sins. Master, pardon our transgressions. Holy One, visit and heal our infirmities, for the glory of Your Name.

Lord, have mercy.(3)

Glory to the Father, and the Son and the Holy Spirit, both now and forever and to the ages of ages. Amen

Our Father, Who art in Heaven, hallowed be Thy name. Thy Kingdom come, Thy will be done, on earth as it is in Heaven. Give us this day our daily bread; and forgive us our trespasses, as we forgive those who trespass against us; and lead us not into temptation, but deliver us from evil.

For Yours is the Kingdom and the Power and the Glory of the Father and the Son and the Holy Spirit, both now and forever and to the ages of ages. Amen.

Psalms
Morning Psalms: 3, 38, 63, 88, 103, 143 — Choose one each day.
Evening Psalms: 70 and 143 — alternate

In morning only:
Commemorate the Living
Lord have mercy on: The leaders of the church, nation, spiritual fathers and mothers, parents and relative, Old and young, needy, orphans, widows, those in sickness and sorrow, those in captivity or confinement. Remember, strengthen and comfort them and grant them speedy relief and freedom and deliverance. (*add your own names*).

Commemorate the Departed
Remember Your servants who have fallen asleep: our grandparents, parents and family members and friends. Forgive them all their sins committed knowingly or unknowingly and grant them Your Kingdom, a portion of Your eternal blessing and the enjoyment of Your unending life. (*add your own names*)

Psalm 51
Have mercy on me, O God, according to Thy great mercy; and according to the multitude of Thy compassions, blot out my transgression. Wash me thoroughly from my iniquity, and cleanse me from my sin. For I realize my iniquity, and my sin is before me continually. (*Pause and remember your sinfulness*) Against Thee only have I sinned I have done evil

in Thy sight, that Thou mayest be justified in Thy words and win when
Thou art judged. For, behold, I was conceived in iniquities, and in sins
did my mother desire me. For, lo, Thou lovest truth; the unknown and
secret things of Thy wisdom Thou hast made known to me. Thou shalt
sprinkle me with hyssop, and I shall be cleansed; Thou shalt wash me,
and I shall become whiter than snow. Thou shalt make me hear joy and
gladness; the bones that have been humbled will rejoice. Turn Thy face
from my sins, and blot out all my iniquities. Create in me a clean heart,
O God; and renew a right spirit within me. Cast me not away from Thy
face, and take not Thy Holy Spirit from me. Restore to me the joy of
Thy salvation, and confirm me with a princely spirit. I shall teach Thy
ways to the lawless and the godless will return to Thee. Deliver me from
blood, O God — O God of my salvation — and my tongue shall extol
Thy justice. O Lord, Thou wilt open my lips, and my mouth shall declare
Thy praise. For if Thou hadst desired sacrifice, I would have given it; but
burnt offerings do not please Thee. The sacrifice for God is a contrite
spirit; a contrite and humble heart God will not despise. Gladden Sion,
O Lord, with Thy good will; and let the walls of Jerusalem be built. Then
Thou wilt be pleased with the sacrifice of righteousness, the oblation and
burnt offerings; then they will offer calves on Thine altar.

The Creed (Symbol of Faith)

I believe in one God, Father, Almighty, Maker of heaven and earth,
and of all things visible and invisible: And in one Lord Jesus Christ,
the only-begotten Son of God; begotten of the Father before all ages;
Light from Light, True God from True God, begotten, not made, of One
Essence with the Father, through Whom all things were made: Who for
us men, and for our salvation, came down from Heaven, and was incar-
nate by the Holy Spirit and the Virgin Mary, and became Man: And was
crucified for us under Pontius Pilate, and suffered and was buried: And
He rose on the third day according to the Scriptures: And ascended into
Heaven, and sits at the right hand of the Father: He will come again with
glory to judge the living and the dead; His Kingdom shall have no end:
And in the Holy Spirit, the Lord, the Creator of the Life, Who proceeds
from the Father, Who with the Father and the Son is equally worshipped
and glorified, Who spoke by the Prophets: And in One, Holy, Catholic

and Apostolic Church. I confess one Baptism for the remission of sins. I look for the Resurrection of the Dead; And the life of the Age to come. Amen.

Lesser Doxology

Glory to God, who has shown us the Light!
Glory to God in the highest, and on earth, peace, good will toward men!
We praise You! We bless You! We worship You!
We glorify You and give thanks to You for Your great glory!

O Lord God, Heavenly King, God the Father Almighty!
O Lord, the Only–begotten Son, Jesus Christ, and the Holy Spirit!
O Lord God, Lamb of God, Son of the Father, Who take away the sins of the world, have mercy on us!

You, Who take away the sins of the world, receive our prayer! You, Who sit on the right hand of the Father, have mercy on us!
For You alone are holy, and You alone are Lord. You alone, O Lord Jesus Christ, are most high in the glory of God the Father! Amen!

I will give thanks to You every day and praise Your Name for ever and ever. Lord, You have been our refuge from generation to generation! I said, "Lord, have mercy on me. Heal my soul, for I have sinned against You!"

Lord, I flee to You, Teach me to do Your will, for You are my God. For with You is the fountain of Life, and in Your light shall we see light. Continue Your lovingkindness to those who know You.

Vouchsafe, O Lord, to keep us this day without sin.
Blessed are You, O Lord, the God of our fathers, and praised and glorified is Your Name forever. Amen.

Let Your mercy be upon us, O Lord, even as we have set our hope on You.

Blessed are You, O Lord; teach me Your statutes.
Blessed are You, O Master; make me to understand Your commandments.
Blessed are You, O Holy One; enlighten me with your precepts.

Your mercy endures forever, O Lord! Do not despise the works of your hands! To You belongs worship, to You belongs praise, to You belongs glory: to the Fa- ther and to the Son and to the Holy Spirit, now and ever and unto ages of ages. Amen.

Morning Prayer of Metropolitan Philaret

Lord, give me the strength to greet the coming day in peace. Help me in all things to rely on Your holy will. Reveal Your will to me every hour of the day. Bless my dealings with all people. Teach me to treat all people who come to me throughout the day with peace of soul and with firm conviction that Your will governs all. In all my deeds and words guide my thoughts and feelings. In unexpected events, let me not forget that all are sent by you. Teach me to act firmly and wisely, without embittering and embarrassing others. Give me the physical strength to bear the labors of this day. Direct my will, teach me to pray, pray in me. Amen.

or Evening Prayer

O Lord, God our Father, if during this day I have sinned in word, deed or thought forgive me in Your goodness and love. Grant me peaceful sleep; protect me from all evil and awake me in the morning that I may glorify you, Your Son and Your Holy Spirit now and forever and ever. Amen.

(*Here you may add your own private prayers using your own words or some of the Prayers found on the Web Page.*)

Jesus prayer — repeat 100 times.
Lord Jesus Christ , Son of God, Have mercy on me a sinner.

Reflection

Reflect quietly on the tasks of the day and prepare yourself for the difficulties you might face, asking God to help.

Dismissal

Glory to the Father and to the Son and to the Holy Spirit, now and ever and unto ages of ages. Amen.

Through the prayers of our holy Fathers, Lord Jesus Christ our God, have mercy on us and save us.

Amen.

Fasting Guidelines

When to Fast

Weekday Fasts
There is the weekly fast on every Wednesday and Friday. We also fast the day before Christmas and Theophany, on the feast days of the Exaltation of the Cross (Sep 14) and the Beheading of John the Baptist (Aug 29).

Fast periods
There are five fasting periods.

1. Great Lent, which lasts for fifty days. Adherence to monastic traditions also calls for a partial fast during the week preceding the beginning of Lent.

2. Holy Week. A lesser fast is observed on the Saturday of Lazarus and Palm Sunday. A strict fast is observed from Holy Monday through the Paschal Vigil.

3. Fast of the Apostles begins on the Monday after the Sunday of All Saints and ends on June 28, the eve of the Feast of Saints Peter and Paul the Apostles. The duration of this fast depends on the date of Pascha; however, in modern usage this fast is not observed with strictness.

4. Fast of the Dormition of the Theotokos (August 1-14).

5. Fast of the Nativity of Christ (November 15-December 24). In modern usage a strict observance of this fast commences after December 12. (The celebration of the Marriage Service which is generally prohibited during fasting periods is permitted between November 15 and December 12).

How to Fast

Strict Fasting
ABSTINENCE OF:
Meat/Meat Products
Dairy Products
Fish/Shell Fish
Olive Oil
Wine

Saturday and Sundays During Fast period
ABSTINENCE OF:
Meat/Meat Products
Dairy Products
Fish
Wine and Oil are allowed.

Feast Days during a fast period
ABSTINENCE OF:
Meat/Meat Products
Dairy Products
Fish, Wine and Oil allowed.

Consult your Spiritual father for appropriate personal fasting guidelines.

For more information about how to
live the Orthodox way of life, visit our website
www.OrthodoxWayofLife.org

or contact Fr. Deacon Charles Joiner at cjoiner@mac.com

or write to Saint George Greek Orthodox Cathedral
406 N Academy St
Greenville, SC, 29601
864-233-8531

www.ingramcontent.com/pod-product-compliance
Lightning Source LLC
Chambersburg PA
CBHW051556120626
46551CB00013B/1543